ZOOM

fun™
with friends

Compiled by Amy E. Sklansky

Little, Brown and Company
Boston   New York   London

First Edition

ZOOM, ZOOMzingers, ZOOMfun, ZOOMerang, ZOOMa Cum Laude, ZOOMmedia,
and all composite ZOOM marks contained herein are trademarks of the WGBH
Educational Foundation.

Library of Congress Cataloging-in-Publication Data

Sklansky, Amy E.
    ZOOMfun with friends / compiled by Amy E. Sklansky — 1st ed.
        p.   cm.
    Summary: A collection of plays, games, party ideas, tips about volunteering,
jokes, and other activities inspired by the television show ZOOM. Features a behind-
the-scenes peek at what goes into filming an episode of ZOOM.
    ISBN 0-316-95275-3
    1. Games — Juvenile literature.   2. Children's plays — Juvenile literature.
3. Children's parties — Juvenile literature.   4. ZOOM (Television program :
WGBH (Television station : Boston, Mass.)) — Juvenile literature. [1. Games.
2. Plays.   3. Parties.]   I. ZOOM (Television program : WGBH
(Television station : Boston, Mass.))   II. Title.   III. Title: ZOOMfun with friends.
GV1203.S564   1999
790.1 — dc21   99-12273

10 9 8 7 6 5 4 3 2 1

Q-KPT
Printed in the United States of America

Funding for ZOOM is provided by
public television viewers,
the National Science Foundation,
and the Corporation for Public Broadcasting.

Design by WGBH

Hey, ZOOMers™

ZOOM™ is TV by kids, for kids.™ **Without you,** there wouldn't be a show! Everything you see on ZOOM was sent in by kids from all over the country.

Each show is a **cool mix** of games, experiments, crafts, kid guests, recipes, brainteasers, jokes, skits, and more. After watching, you'll want to try all the activities yourself.

But ZOOM is more than TV. We have a Web site at **www.pbs.org/zoom** and our own newsletter called ZOOMerang.™ So check us out when you're surfing the Internet. Send us your ideas by mail or e-mail, and we'll send you the latest edition of ZOOMerang and consider putting your ideas on the show.

For now, though, we've come up with a book full of different ways to have **fun with your friends.** Included are tips for throwing a party, plays from the ZOOMplayhouse, ZOOMgames,™ ideas about how you and your friends can make a difference in your community, guest features, jokes, wacky facts, and more.

You might recognize some of your favorite things from TV, but you'll find lots of **new stuff,** too, including a peek at what goes on behind the scenes at ZOOM. You'll also find some top secret tips about how to create your own secret code and how to make invisible ink.

So turn the page and **c'mon and have some ZOOMfun™** with your friends!

Alisa
Keiko
Lynese
Zoe
David
Pablo
Jared

P.S. **Check out** the last page to find out how to send your ideas to ZOOM.

Contents

whatZup!

ZOOMguest™

whatZup!

Make a Difference

Top Secret Stuff

Everything You Always Wanted to Know about ZOOM

Hubi! Ubare yubou rubeaduby fubor subome fubun?

What? You can't understand what I'm saying? That's because I'm speaking Ubbi Dubbi, ZOOM's secret language. We promise to reveal the secret to speaking Ubbi Dubbi before this book ends — so keep reading!

Throw a Party!

What's more fun with friends than a party?

There are lots of different kinds of parties, of course — birthdays, celebrations of special events, holidays, and more.

Do you have a birthday soon? How about a friend or a family member? Is it close to your favorite holiday? Do you feel like throwing a party for no reason at all?

Well, we've included some tips for partying the ZOOM! way.

Read on and you'll find out that planning a party can be almost as fun as the party itself!

Pick a theme.
A theme can tie a party together. For instance, if your theme is Halloween your invitations might have monsters on them, your menu might be spooky-sounding, your cake might be in the shape of a pumpkin, and party games could include "Pin the Tail on the Witch's Black Cat."

A theme can be anything you like:

holidays, the circus, sports, spring, fairy tales, or a TV show.

Make Invitations

Key things to include in an invitation are:

Who (party host or hostess)
What (kind of party)
Where (party location)
When (date and time)

Be creative in making your invitations. They can reflect the theme of your party or just look like fun.

Before you start, make sure you have the proper size envelopes for your invitations. Or you could make an invitation that can be folded in half and stapled. In this case, be sure to leave the back side blank so you can address and stamp the invitation.

You might also make postcards or hand-deliver the invitations. One fun way to decorate invitations is to create your own stamped design.

(See the facing page.)

4

Rubber Band Stamps

You will **need:**

- cardboard
- scissors
- double-sided tape
- rubber bands
  (an assortment of widths)
- stamp pads with washable
  ink or washable markers
- paper

Cut a piece of cardboard the right size for your stamp. Then cut some rubber bands and arrange them in a design on top of the cardboard.

Tape on the rubber bands using the double-sided tape. Make sure the rubber band pieces do not overlap, or parts of your design won't show up when you print. Cut pieces of paper in the size and shape you want for your invitations.

Press your stamp onto the stamp pad or color each piece of rubber band with the markers. Press the stamp onto a blank invitation.

P.S. If you want to spell something on your stamp, be sure to spell it backwards (the way it looks in the mirror) because the printing process reverses the letters.

Sent in by
Becca S. of
Livingston,
New Jersey.

More Invitation Tips

Mail or deliver your invitations about **three weeks** before the party, or far enough in advance so that people will not make other plans.

If you mail your invitations, make sure you know the **right amount of postage** to use. Large or square invitations often cost more to mail. Take an invitation to the post office and have it weighed to find out the correct postage.

You might choose to end your invitation with the letters **R.S.V.P.,** which stands for the French phrase **"répondez s'il vous plaît."** This basically means **"Please let your host or hostess know whether or not you can come."** Underneath R.S.V.P., write your phone number and the date by which you'd like to know if your guests can attend (one week before the party should be fine).

Plan the Party Menu at Cafe ZOOM

Sent in by John K. of Womelsdorf, Pennsylvania; Jon B. of Camden, Arizona; and Taquilla M. of Joliet, Illinois.

Pizza Bagels

You will **need:**
- bagels
- tomato sauce
- shredded cheese
- any other toppings you like (mushrooms, onions, green pepper)

Ask an adult to **cut** the bagels in half and help you with the oven.

Preheat the oven to **375** degrees. Place the bagels on a baking sheet covered with foil. Spread a spoonful of **sauce** on each bagel half. Add other **toppings** if desired. Next, sprinkle the **cheese** on top. Carefully place the baking sheet in the oven and bake for about **10** minutes or until the cheese melts.

Cool and enjoy!

Here's a **joke** from Kelly F. of Saint Claire Shores, Michigan:

How do you fix a broken pizza??

Answer: With tomato paste.

First make the pudding according to the instructions on the box. Then crush the cookies into small bits using the back of the wooden spoon. Stir the cookie bits into the pudding — **this is your dirt!**

If you'd like to use flower pot containers for your dirt pudding, make sure they are clean. Then line the bottoms with foil so that your pudding doesn't leak out the bottom.

Pour the pudding mixture into the flower pots or cups. Top off your dirt pudding by adding some **Gummi worms** and a **fake flower.** Enjoy!

You will need:

- **chocolate pudding (We used the instant kind.)**
- **chocolate wafer cookies**
- **a wooden spoon**
- **cups or small plastic flower pots**
- **aluminum foil**
- **Gummi worms and/or fake flowers**

Dirt Pudding

Sent in by Kevin W. of Charleston, South Carolina.

Bunny Cake

You will need:

- store-bought cake mix or homemade (enough for two 8-inch round cakes)
- ingredients needed for cake mix — see the back of the box (usually eggs, vegetable oil, and water)
- 2 round 8-inch cake pans
- I can of frosting — the main color for your bunny
- tubes of decorating frosting
- candy decorations, such as jelly beans, sprinkles, licorice, or M&M's
- a big tray for serving

Ask an adult for help when using the oven.

First make the cake batter according to instructions on the box. Then **bake the batter** in two greased 8-inch cake pans. Allow the cakes to cool completely on a rack, about two to three hours.

One cake will be the **face of the bunny** — set it aside. Cut ears and a bow tie out of the other cake. Then assemble the cake on the tray so that it looks like a bunny.

Frost the entire cake. (Don't forget the sides!) Then, with a tube of decorating frosting, outline the ears and bow tie. Use jelly beans for eyes, licorice for whiskers, and other candy for **decorating** the tie.

Sent in by Will T. of Brookline, Massachusetts.

Cupcakes

Make cupcakes using a store-bought cake mix or homemade. **Decorate** them according to your theme using sprinkles, M&M's, licorice, cinnamon candies, and even pipe cleaners. For instance, if you're having a **Halloween** party, you could turn a chocolate cupcake into a **spider** by adding some black pipe cleaner legs.

Upside-Down Ice Cream Faces

Put a scoop of ice cream on a plate and put a sugar cone on top of it, so it looks like a hat. **Decorate** the ice cream scoop using frosting and/or candy to look like a face — funny or scary, depending on your party theme.

Hey, Alisa

Yeah, Pablo?

If you could have anything named after you, what would it be?

A curly-haired, freckled doll that laughs when you pull the string.

Cran-Ras Ginger Ale

You will need:
cranberry raspberry juice
ginger ale
ice

Pour juice into a pitcher. Then pour in the same amount of ginger ale. Add ice cubes. Drink up!

Is all this reading about food making you thirsty? Try this:

Juicy Cubes

Make some fun and fancy ice cubes by freezing various juices in your ice trays. Or, you can freeze a cherry inside each cube. These colored cubes look really great when served in clear sodas and clear cups.

Funky Fruit Faces

You will need:
**fruit or vegetables
(apples, green peppers,
potatoes, pears,
or oranges)
toothpicks
marshmallows or
gumdrops
raisins or other
dried fruit, such as
cranberries or apricots**

Create funky fruit faces by attaching the marshmallows, candy, or dried fruits to the fruits or vegetables by using toothpicks or pieces of toothpicks. Arrange in a group in the center of the table.

Note: If you decide to eat your centerpiece later, remember to remove the toothpicks first!

If you're looking for some fruit face inspiration, check out Play With Your Food by Joost Elffers (Stewart, Tabori, and Chang, Inc.)

Play these ZOOM games™ at your Party

Bob for Apples

You will **need:**
- a **basin** filled with water
- an **apple** for everyone in your group
- a **towel**

Float the apples in the basin. With your hands behind your back, lean over and try to **grab an apple** using only your **teeth.**

Hint:
If the apple has a stem, sometimes that's an easy way to grab it.

Or try this in midair!

You will **need:**
- several pieces of **string**
- an **apple** for everyone in your group

Tie one string to the stem of an apple. Then fasten the other end of the string somewhere that will allow the apple to hang freely, such as above a doorway. The apple needs to hang down to about the level of your chin. Repeat with the other apples.

Now put your hands behind your back and try to take a bite out of an apple. **You can do it!**

Zfact:

According to the *Guinness Book of Records 1996*, the largest apple ever grown weighed **3 pounds, 2 ounces.** How would you like to bob for *that* apple?!

Suitcase Relay

Sent in by Kirsten J. of Bozeman, Montana.

You will need:
two suitcases packed with shirts, sweaters, hats, scarves, etc. Each suitcase should contain the same number of items.

Form **two teams.** Place the two suitcases at the finish line.

At **"Go!"** one player from each team runs to a suitcase, opens it, and **puts on** every single item in the suitcase.

When **finished,** the player shuts the suitcase and **runs** with it back to the starting line.

At the **starting line,** the player **removes** all the items, puts them back in the suitcase, and closes it. Then he or she **runs** with the suitcase back to the finish line and leaves it there.

Then the player **returns** once more to the starting line and **tags** a teammate. This player should do the same thing. The first team to finish **wins.**

Fannee Doolee

likes **apples** but not **fruit.** Why do you think that is?

What will fashion and music be like 100 years from now?

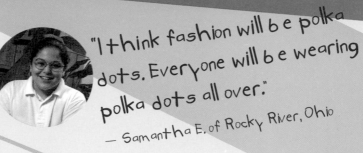

"I think fashion will be polka dots. Everyone will be wearing polka dots all over."
— Samantha E. of Rocky River, Ohio

"Clothes will be really different and weird and baggy—music will be country and rap mixed together and sound really funky."
— Jasleen S. of Rockville, Maryland

"Automatic drying button for clothes and TV screens in jackets."
— Paul B. of Rockville, Maryland

"Fashion will be like 'Back to the Future' with hover boards and there will be jackets that clean themselves and music will be a higher type of rap."
— Tim B. of Silver Spring, Maryland

"People dressing fancier, higher shoes, more classical music."
— Alexandra S. of Silver Spring, Maryland

What do you think ??

You will need:

- balloons
- cardboard tubes (from paper towels or toilet paper)
- newspaper (in long strips about 2" wide)
- masking tape
- flour
- water
- colored tissue paper
- white craft glue
- scissors
- paint (optional)
- string
- hole puncher
- wrapped candies and small toys
- confetti (optional)
- blindfold
- plastic bat

Plan ahead because your piñata will need several days to dry.

Mexican Piñata

Zfact:

Piñatas

are favorites at all kinds of celebrations—from birthdays to Cinco de Mayo. Cinco de Mayo means the Fifth of May and is a national holiday in Mexico. On May 5, Mexicans celebrate their victory over the French at the Battle of Puebla on May 5, 1862. This battle was an important step in the fight for Mexican independence. Today, this holiday is celebrated with fiestas and parades.

Use the balloons and cardboard tubes to form any shape of piñata you want. For example, if you'd like to make a dog, you would start by blowing up two different-sized balloons— one for its body and one for its head. With the tape, attach cardboard tubes for the legs. Cut two small pieces of cardboard and tape them onto the smaller balloon to make ears.

In a large bowl, mix 1 1/2 cups flour with 1 cup water until the mixture looks similar to pancake batter. If you run out of this paste, make a new batch.

Dip a newspaper strip into the bowl, making sure the entire strip gets wet. Remove excess liquid by pulling the wet strip through two fingers. Then, drape and smooth the strips over the figure, slightly overlapping each strip. Do this until you have completely covered your figure three times. Then cover the figure with a dry layer of strips. (They will stick to the last wet layer if you work quickly enough.)

Wait several days until your piñata is completely dry. Then decorate it by gluing on strips of tissue paper to make layers of colored fringe. If you like, you can attach a tail made of paper or string and paint on a face or other details.

Cut a small flap in the top of your piñata and pop the balloon. Pour in wrapped candies and small toys, such as plastic rings, small yo-yos, or small rubber balls. (You can also pour in confetti, which you can make yourself with a hole puncher and colored paper.) Close the flap.

Punch a couple of holes in the top of your piñata and attach a string for hanging. Hang the piñata so that your guests can reach it by swinging a bat.

Blindfold one of your guests and ask them to spin around three times. Then hand them the bat and point them toward the piñata. Guests should take turns hitting the piñata until someone breaks it open. When this happens, everyone scrambles for the goodies!

15

Act 1t Out!

Have you ever wanted to **act in a play?** How about sing or dance onstage? Maybe clown around in a circus? **In this section** you will find plays written by kids that you and your friends can star in. Maybe they'll even inspire you to write your own play. If so, send it to ZOOM. You'll also find some features starring showstopping ZOOMguests.

Before you enter the ZOOMplayhouse, here are some terms that you might want to know:

script: text of the play

cast: the characters in the play

set: the scenery for the stage

props: objects used by actors during the play, such as a magic wand or a cane

"curtain up": the start of a performance

"break a leg": To actors this phrase means "good luck." Why? No one knows for sure. It may be that superstitious actors think that if they wish one thing, the opposite will come true. So, telling an actor to "break a leg" is really wishing him or her the best of luck.

This ticket is redeemable just by turning the page.

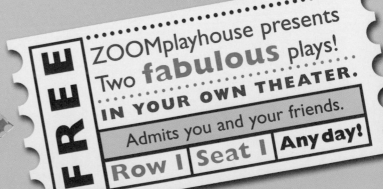

FREE

ZOOMplayhouse presents Two **fabulous** plays! **IN YOUR OWN THEATER.** Admits you and your friends.

| Row I | Seat I | Any day! |

16

Meet Tristan, Patrick, and Sarah

Three Friends Who Like to Clown Around

Q: How old are you?
Sarah: I'm 13 years old.
Tristan: I'm 13 years old.
Patrick: I'm 12 years old.

Q: How did you learn about clowning?
A: We're spending the summer at Circus Smirkus in Greensboro, Vermont. We train in a circus barn for two weeks and then we tour around New England. Part of being at the circus is being a clown, and part of being a clown is doing makeup.

Q: What do you like about being a clown?
Patrick: When I started clowning I was very shy. And when I put on makeup they really didn't know who I was. Then I came to Circus Smirkus, and I'm really not shy anymore.
Tristan: Putting on clown makeup kind of makes me hyper. I can be sad or I can be happy.
Sarah: When I put on makeup I know my personality totally changes. I sort of get a jump of energy because I know that I'll make people happy, which makes me happy, too.

Q: Is there any makeup advice you could give to aspiring clowns?
A: Sure. We use professional-quality makeup called "grease paint," but you can use the face paints you can buy in any toy store.

makeup advice

1. Put on the white first.
2. Next, put on the red.
3. Put on the black last.
   Go slow so the colors don't run.

The Elevator

by the ZOOMers

The Cast

SUSANNA STAR, a vain, self-important movie star
BILL COWHOON, a humble dairy farmer
CATHY, a young woman who talks nonstop
FAN, a young fan of Susanna Star
NEW PERSON, a random elevator passenger

Costumes

Feather boa and movie star glasses for SUSANNA STAR
Cowboy hat for BILL COWHOON

Props

Handbag containing mirror, comb, lipstick, and nail file
(for SUSANNA STAR); briefcase with picture of a cow on it
(for BILL COWHOON); camera (for FAN).

Set   An office elevator.

[**Fan** *tries to take a photo of* **Susanna Star** *as she enters the elevator.*]

Star: Enough! I don't want to be late meeting my movie agent! Let's see — Floor 17.

[*The doors close.* **Susanna** *is alone. She strikes some funny, show-offy poses and admires herself in a mirror. The elevator stops.* **Bill Cowhoon** *and* **Cathy** *step on.*]

Bill Cowhoon: Evening, ma'ams!

Cathy (to Bill)**:** Can you press 18, please?
[*The elevator starts to go up.*]

Cathy (to Bill)**:** Are you from out of town?

Bill Cowhoon: Well, I . . .

[**Susanna** *takes out mirror and admires herself again.*]

Cathy: Because I'm from out of town, too. I mean not too far out of town. Just a little out of town.

Susanna Star: Enough! Your chatter is giving me a headache!

Cathy: Really? Do you think I talk a lot? I don't think I talk a lot! I think I talk just enough. That's why I like elevators because you can always find someone to talk to —

Bill Cowhoon: Cows.

Susanna Star: I beg your pardon?

Bill Cowhoon: I live out of town, milking cows. I am president of the Cow Milking Association. It's a very serious business.

*[**Susanna** uses makeup items.]*

Cathy: Really? Wow!! I've never milked a COW before. Of course I've heard a cow moo before. I think cows moo as much as I talk. Don't you?

Susanna Star: Enough! I must concentrate on breathing so I may inhale the beauty and exhale the wrinkles. I can't afford any wrinkles. One, two, three. One, two, three…*[The elevator stops suddenly and everyone is jolted.]*

All: AHHHH!!!

Cathy: The elevator's not moving! Let me try the buttons! *[She furiously presses the elevator buttons.]*

Bill Cowhoon: Allow me — these are very experienced milking hands! *[He methodically tries the elevator buttons.]*

Continued on next page

Susanna Star: Enough, let me try the phone. Hello, anyone there? It's me, Susanna Star, the most beautiful, ageless star of all Hollywood.

moo!

Cathy: Give me that! Hello, this is Cathy. Can I ask you a question? Do you think I talk a lot? I really don't think I do but I thought I'd take a survey just to find out if —

Bill Cowhoon: What are you doing? We are stuck in an elevator, for Pete's sake — ask for some help.

Cathy: It's dead.

Susanna Star: Enough! Try something else. How about the elevator door?

moo!

Bill Cowhoon: Good idea!

[**Bill** *elaborately prepares to open the door and then moos like a cow.*] Moo…moo…moo.
[**Cathy** *and* **Susanna** *look at him strangely.*]

Bill Cowhoon: I find mooing helps the body and the mind. It keeps my cows eternally young, especially Bessie.

Susanna Star: Really? Eternally young? One, two, three, mooo…One, two, three, mooo…

[**Susanna** *tries a few more moos.*]

Cathy: One, two, three, mooo…one, two, three, mooo…

Bill Cowhoon: It's not working. My cows would be so ashamed. The Cow Milking Association will never allow me to

milk another cow again. *[continual mooing cries]*
Moo-hoo, moo-hoo…

*[**Cathy** chatters on.]*

Susanna Star: Must keep breathing. Stars
can't have wrinkles! *[She pulls out mirror and screams.]*
Oh, no! A wrinkle. I can't have a wrinkle. Maybe some more
mooing would help! *[She begins mooing.]*

Cathy: This is great! Stuck
in an elevator means that I have
a captive audience! I can talk to
them as long as I want.

Bill Cowhoon: We're doomed!
I'll never see Bessie the Cow again!

Susanna Star: What about my
fans? My wrinkles?

Cathy: What if I run out of things to say?

All: DOOMED!!!!!! *[The elevator moves, everyone is jolted again.]*

All: It's working!

*[**All** straighten themselves out and are quiet. When the doors open,
Susanna and **Bill** exit.]*

Bill Cowhoon: So long, ma'ams.

Susanna Star: Enough!

*[**Cathy** stays as **New Person** joins her.]*

Cathy: Do you think I talk a lot? I don't. I just love elevators!
I could talk and ride in them all day long!! Couldn't you?

The End

Meet Audrey
and Find Out Why She Likes to Dance

Q: How old are you?
Audrey: I'm eleven.

Q: Why do you dance?
Audrey: I dance because it makes me feel great. Dancing is the sort of communication that lets me express myself without talking. I think dance really is someone's mood or whoever choreographs the dance. If they're happy, they'll make it an upbeat dance. It can be a mix of everything.

Q: Describe dance practice.
Audrey: Practice is every Saturday at 9:45 and lasts about five hours. Right now, we're rehearsing the "Subway" piece for our year-end performance, which this year is called "City, City." We usually just polish all the steps until they're really perfect.

Q: What's your role in the piece?
Audrey: In the subway piece, I don't have the lead — I'm in the chorus. My best friend has the lead. I think she's a really great dancer, and she thinks I'm a great dancer. Different people need to get different parts sometimes.

Q: Do you think you'll keep dancing as you get older?
Audrey: The National Dance Institute is one of the best things that's ever happened to me. I think it's made me appreciate dance more. I think that's the kind of thing that's going to stay with me for all my life.

ZOOMplayhouse™

Written by Jessica F.
of Wellesley, Massachusetts.

Happily Ever After?

The Cast

Prince Charming
a dashing young prince

Cindy
the prince's new bride, formerly Cinderella

Sylvia
Cindy's mean, lazy stepsister

Fran
Cindy's other mean, lazy stepsister

Mother
mother to Sylvia and Fran, step-mother to Cindy

Costumes: **Cindy** *and* **Prince Charming** *should both wear crowns and elegant royal clothing; the others should look nice, but not as fancy.*

Props: bucket and scrub brush or sponge; throne, three chairs for guests.

Setting: castle interior

[As the play opens, **Cindy** *is sitting on the throne looking sad.]*

Prince: What's the matter, Cindy?

Cindy: Oh, Charming. Call me a creature of habit but I just can't stand sitting still like this. I need…I need…

Prince: What? What?

Cindy: A…a…bucket!

Prince: A bucket?

Cindy: A bucket. And a sponge… and some soap.

Prince: For cryin' out loud, Cindy — here's your bucket!!

[**Prince** *takes out bucket from behind throne; then the doorbell rings.*]

Prince: Oh, that must be your stepmother and stepsisters coming for tea.

[**Prince** *puts down bucket, crosses to door, opens it, and greets his new in-laws.*]

Cindy *(sarcastically)***:** Oh, great. Now I have to put on my charming hostess act.

[**Cindy** *breaks into fake smile and stands to greet her family.*]

Mother! Sylvia! Fran! How lovely to see you!

Sylvia: I'm sure. Cindy, you must come home. Ever since you left, I've had to do all the washing. I've just been sooo tired.

Fran: Me, too. Now that I have to do all the cooking, my arms are as limp as my spaghetti.

Sylvia: *You* do all the cooking? *I* do all the cooking!

Fran: Do not.

Sylvia: Do too.

Fran: Do not.

Sylvia: *Do too!!!*

Cindy: Oh, pul-ease!

Prince *(to his guests)***:** Would you still do those things even if you lived in the palace with me?

[**Fran** *and* **Sylvia** *are fighting in the background.*]

Mother: Absolutely not. My girls couldn't waste their time doing such exhausting things. That would be wasting their precious energy. No, my beauties would be good little queens.

Cindy *(yawning)***:** Excuse me, but I think I'll go mow the lawn.

[*She starts to exit but* **Prince** *interrupts.*]

Prince: Wait a second, Cinders! Go back to your attic where you happily slave away all day! We're getting a divorce!

Mother: A divorce? You can't just split after being married for only a day! You've got to give it some time. As a matter of fact, what time is it? I'm missing my soaps.

Prince: I've already found the perfect queens! Sylvia? Fran? Will you marry me?

[**Cindy** begins dusting.]

Sylvia/**Fran:** What? What are you talking about?

Prince: Cindy can't sit still for three seconds. She keeps cleaning and cleaning and cleaning! I need someone who can be a good queen — patient, proper…and lazy!

[on his knees]

Please, marry me! Pretty please with sugar and a cherry on top?

Sylvia (looking at Fran): Sugar?!

Fran (looking at Sylvia): Cherry?!

[**Both** wiggle over to **Prince** and smile at him.]

Prince: So, whaddaya say?

Sylvia/**Fran:** Maraschino!!!
[They hook arms with **Prince** and walk up an aisle.]

Prince (turns to Cindy): See ya later, Cindy!!!

Mother (jumping up): Wait! I'm lazy, too! Charming!

[**Mother** runs after them.]

Cindy (moping): Oh great, now what am I supposed to do?

[She sees bucket and soap in corner.]

Well, no use leaving a dirty palace.

[She starts cleaning an imaginary wall.]

The End

Maybe you'd like to put on a show, but you'd rather do it on a smaller stage — where you can be in charge of acting, directing, lighting, and set and costume design all at the same time. **Welcome to:**

Shadow Puppet Theater

The PUPPET

- First, use the chalk or pencil to **draw the outline** of an animal or a person on the poster board. Then draw its features, such as eyes, nose, mouth, stripes, or spots.
- **Cut out** the figure and all of its features (so the eyes, etc., are now holes).
- Now turn your puppet over so that the back is facing up, and tape over the cut-out features with **colored tissue paper,** as shown.
- If you want certain parts of your puppet's body to be movable, such as an arm or a tail, draw and cut them out separately. Attach the **moving parts** to the puppet with the brass fasteners.
- Now, tape or **glue** one of the unsharpened pencils or sticks to the back of the puppet and any movable body parts. Set your puppet aside.

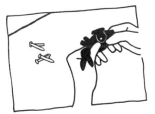

Sent in by the students of Citizen Schools in Boston, Massachusetts

The THEATER

You'll also need:
- a cardboard box big enough for a few puppet performers
- white tissue paper
- reading lamp or flashlight

- **Cut** all the flaps off the box. **Cut** out one of the long sides of the box. **Cut** a large rectangle out of the other long side.
- Cover the cut-out rectangle from the inside with white tissue paper and tape it around the edges. Be sure the tissue is pulled tight and smooth. This will be your **backdrop.** Decorate the rest of the outside of the box like a theater, if you like.
- Place a reading **lamp or flashlight** so that it shines directly behind the tissue-paper (backstage) side of the box. Turn off all other lights.
- Then hold your puppet against the back of the tissue-paper side of the box. The light should **shine on** the back side of your puppets and right through all of the colored features. This will make your shadow puppets look stunning to the audience.

Make more puppets and put on a show for your friends. **Or teach** your friends how to make puppets and put on a show together.

Zfact:

Hombres Chinoises (Chinese Shadow Show)
was a very popular form of entertainment with eighteenth-century French royalty. The directions on these pages are very similar to those followed in France nearly 300 years ago. You may want to consider performing a French fairy tale favorite, such as "Le petit chaperon rouge" (Little Red Riding Hood).

The Hand Shadow Zoo

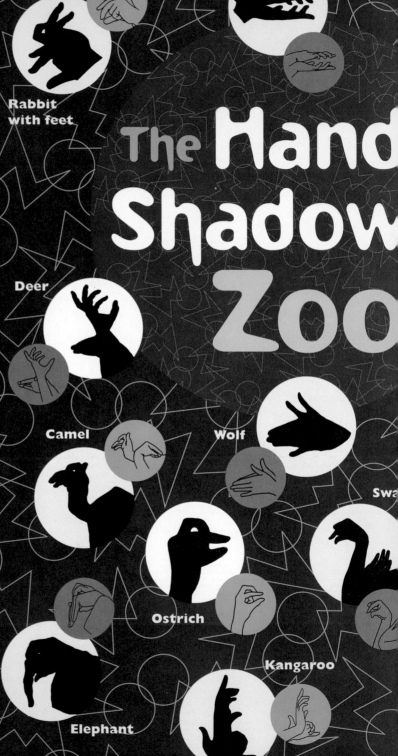

Simple rabbit

Rabbit with feet

Alligator

Deer

Camel

Wolf

Swa

Ostrich

Elephant

Kangaroo

Ever wish you could invite an elephant into your room or a kangaroo into your kitchen? You can!

Hand shadows are another way you and your friends can put on a performance. Try making some of the animals on these pages. If you change the position of your fingers slightly you can make the animals come alive by opening and closing their mouths or eyes, wiggling an ear, and so on. Practice doing this with sound effects, and you'll have the whole zoo howling, talking, and singing in no time.

Write your own hand shadow play. Act out a fairy tale with your own twist. Or your hand shadow could sing a funny song — maybe even a duet with a friend's hand shadow.

All you need is a single light source (like a flashlight or reading lamp) behind you and a clear wall in front of you.

Shadows

A Poem

The sun has risen!
The shadows appear!
They move where you move,
They hear what you hear.
The dark is rising,
Your shadows fade,
They follow your footsteps,
As if they are made.

Z fact:

Bunraku is a form of puppetry practiced in Japan. This puppet tradition dates back to the ninth century. Bunraku puppets are about two-thirds life-size and have no strings. Traditionally, a team of three men work together to move the puppet. One man moves the feet. Another moves the left arm. The most senior man stands on stilt-like shoes and moves the right arm and the head. It takes many years to learn to become a Bunraku operator.

The puppet's words are spoken by a chanter who sits to the audience's right, next to the musician who plays the samisen (a Japanese instrument that looks a little like a long-necked guitar) for the puppet's many musical numbers.

Meet Aaron

and Get a Glimpse of Life as a Recording Artist

Q: How old are you?
A: I'm ten years old.

Q: When did you know you wanted to be a singer?
A: I've wanted to be a singer since I was very, very little.

Q: How did you get started in your musical career?
A: The first thing I did was ask my mom if I could take singing lessons.

Q: What's it like to be on the road?
A: My mom comes on tour with me. I feel like I'm at home. We have a tour bus. I have a bunk bed that I sleep in when I feel like it.

Q: What do you like to do when you're not onstage?
A: I horse around like other kids do. And when I'm on the road, I love to play football.

Q: What's your favorite part of being a performer?
A: My favorite part is meeting the fans and giving them my autograph.

Q: Do you think you will continue to perform as you get older?
A: Going onstage is completely the best thing. I love this job so much I'm always going to be doing this, all my life.

Fun and Games!

In this section you'll find all kinds of games — games you can play with friends at school or at home, inside or outside. You can also learn how to make a Fortune-teller to amaze your friends.

But remember, when you play games it's not about whether you win or lose — it's all about having fun with your friends. Let the games begin!

Sent in by Crys N. of Mt. Vernon, Maine.

Stand in a circle and turn so you're facing the back of the player next to you.

Scoot really close together and try to sit on the lap of the player behind you.

Can you do this **without falling over?** How long before there's a "pile up"?

P.S. For an added challenge, try singing "Row, Row, Row Your Boat" three times before a "pile up" occurs.

Pile Up!

Fannee Doolee likes **blizzards** but doesn't like **snow.** Why do you think that is?

Shoe Relay

Janine L. of McLean, Virginia, and Heidi N. of Currie, North Carolina, both sent in this game.

After players take off their shoes and **mix them up** in a pile, form two teams.

At "Go!" one player from each team runs to the pile, finds his or her shoes, puts them on, and **ties them.**

Next, the player runs back to the team and tags the next player on his or her team. Then the **tagged player runs** to the pile and does the same thing. Repeat until all players are wearing shoes. The first team to finish **wins.**

P.S. You can make this game **tougher** by tying some of the pairs of shoes together.

Sneakers a poem

I love my sneakers, I really do
In fact I think they're the best kind of shoe
They are kind of dirty
But so is my dog Fergie
They are not high tops
And they do not have dots
But there is a cool star on the side
They work great when I have to run and hide
They feel good when I walk around
I think they're the best pair in town.
My sneakers are really neat
I'm so glad they're on my feet.

Sent in by Liza C. of Beverly, Massachusetts.

What has a tongue but cannot talk?

Answer: A shoe.

Sock Steal

First **take off your shoes** and set them aside.

Then pull your socks down so that they are **flopping** and **hanging** off your toes.

Now crawl around on your hands and knees and **try to steal** the other players' socks.

When both of your socks have been stolen, you're out. The **winner** is the last one left wearing a sock.

Hey, Jared.
Yeah, Keiko?
If you could have anything named after you, what would it be?
A soda brand.

33

Octopus Tag
[Uboctubopubus Tubag]

This game was sent in by Julie H. of Three Oaks, Michigan, who says, "The more people you have, the more fun you'll have!"

Choose one person to be **"It."** The person who is "It" chases everyone, as in regular tag.

However, whenever "It" **tags** someone, "It" joins hands with the tagged person.

Now the two players tag as a group. Every time someone new is tagged, he or she **joins** the chain. The last person to be tagged is the winner.

Here's a **joke** from Averie A. of the San Dieguito Boys & Girls Club of Solana Beach, California:

What did the boy octopus say to the girl octopus?

Answer: I want to hold your hand, hand, hand, hand, hand, hand, hand, hand.

Zfact: In Nigeria this game is called "Da Ga," which means "The Big Snake." Do you see why?

Sent in by the students of Citizen Schools in Boston, Massachusetts.

The Wind Blows

This game is a little like "Musical Chairs" but without the music. It can help you get to know your friends a little better, too.

Find a chair for everyone but one player, who is the leader. Ask the players to put their chairs in a circle and sit down. The leader stands in the middle of the circle.

The leader starts a sentence with "The wind blows to anyone who ..." and then adds something like "is wearing green," or "has a sister," or "likes ice cream."

Then each player who has the mentioned characteristic gets up from his or her chair and runs to sit in an empty one.

The player left without a chair stands in the middle and is the new leader. He or she begins again with "The wind blows to anyone who ..."

zfact: According to the *Guinness Book of Records 1996*, the windiest place in the world is Commonwealth Bay, in Antarctica, where the wind reaches 200 miles per hour. Hold on to your hat!

If you could have any kind of **pet,** what would it be and why?

Art sent in by Michelle J. of Cedar Rapids, Iowa.

"I would want an elephant because it's big and would annoy my mom."

Alet M. of Silver Spring, Maryland

"A white tiger because they're my favorite."

Kate K. of Potomac, Maryland

"A green iguana because they look cool and they're neat."

Tim B. of Silver Spring, Maryland

"A black lab puppy because they're cute and sweet."

Rachel N. of Silver Spring, Maryland

"Tropical fish because they are neat and I would study them."

Paul B. of Rockville, Maryland

How about you ??

"A horse because I like riding and my favorite book is *Black Beauty*."

Emily S. of Silver Spring, Maryland

Funny Bones

Choose one player to be the leader. Everyone else should form **pairs.**

When the leader calls out a command to **match** body parts, each pair **acts** it out. For example, if the command were "knee to hip," one player would touch his or her knee to the partner's hip. It's up to the partners to decide who carries out which part of the command.

Then the leader continues calling out **commands,** like "hand to elbow" or "shoulder to head."

The pair must remain standing as they act out the commands. If a pair falls, they're out. The last pair left holding the position and **still standing** is the winner.

P.S. If you're getting pretty good at this game, try these tougher commands: "elbow to foot," "nose to shin," and "knee to back."

Hubow dubo
yubou mubake uba
skubelubetubon
lubaugh?

Answer: Tub ikkle ub it s
fub unnnb y ub one.

zfacts

The **funny bone** is really a nerve that tingles whenever you bump it.

The game "Follow the Leader" and its many variations have been played by children since the twelfth century.

Caterpillars:
A Round
Written by Alisa

Caterpillars,
Different Colors,
In the Leaves.
Different Sizes,
On the Trees.

Creepy,

Crawly,

Nibbling,

Munching.

Caterpillars,
On the Ground
Different Patterns
All Around,
Different
Directions.

Fuzzy,

Bright,

Quick,

Slow.

Caterpillars.

Caterp

"I had fun writing this poem because rounds are fun to do with friends. Here's how it works: One person starts off reading and just reads through the whole poem. The second person starts reading at the beginning when the first person starts the verse Caterpillars, On the Ground and then continues all the way through. Once the first person stops reading it through, he or she repeats the first verse again — this way both people end at the same time on the word caterpillars. By the way, when you see a gap between lines, this means you should pause for a second."

illar Relay

You will need two large balls, such as soccer balls or beach balls. After you play this game, see if you can figure out why this is called **Caterpillar Relay.**

Split into two teams and form two single-file lines parallel to each other.

At "Go!" the first **player** in each line passes the ball overhead to the person directly behind. Then the second player in each line **passes the ball** between his or her legs to the player directly behind. Keep **alternating** in this fashion until the ball reaches the last player in line.

The player who gets **the ball** last runs to the front of the line and begins the pattern again. This is repeated until every player has been at the front of the line one time. The first team to finish wins.

Sent in by Mario D. of San Francisco, California.

How to Make a Fortune-Teller

You will need one *square* piece of paper.

1 Fold the paper in half and then open it up. Fold it in half in the other direction and open it up. The point at which the folds cross each other is the exact middle of the paper.

2 Fold each corner to the middle of the paper.

3 Turn the paper over, and fold the corners to the middle of the paper.

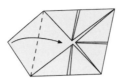

4 Turn the paper back over so that you are looking at four flaps of paper. Color each flap a different color or write the name of a different color on each flap.

5 Turn the Fortune-teller over again and write the numbers 1 to 8 on the eight triangles of paper.

6 Lift each numbered flap and write a funny fortune under each number. You might write things like "You will grow up to be a famous opera singer," "Tomorrow will be your lucky day," or "True love is in your future."

Fortune-teller

Sent in by Kelly H. of Provincetown, Massachusetts.

Telling Fortunes

1 Fold your Fortune-teller in half with the colors on the outside. Open it up and fold it in half in the other direction. Insert your fingers underneath the colored flaps.

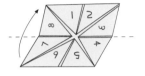

2 Pinch your index finger and thumb together to open the Fortune-teller one way. To open it the other way, press your two thumbs and two index fingers together.

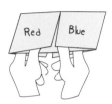

3 Close the Fortune-teller and ask your friend to pick a color. Then spell the color out loud, opening your Fortune-teller in alternating directions for each letter. (For example, you would open the Fortune-teller five times for "green.") Leave the Fortune-teller open on the last letter.

4 Ask your friend to pick a number. Count to that number while opening and closing your Fortune-teller. Leave the Fortune-teller open on the number.

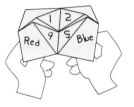

5 Ask your friend to pick another number. Lift the flap of that number and reveal your friend's fortune!

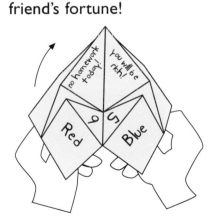

Wink!

Sent in by Bonnie K. of Pittsboro, North Carolina.

You will need **paper and a pencil.**

Tear one small piece of paper for every player.
Write a **"Z"** on one piece. Leave the others blank. Fold all the pieces and place them in a bowl or hat.

Ask each player to draw a piece of paper and look at it **without letting anyone else see** if there is anything written on it.

The person who draws the **"Z"** is the **Winker,** but the Winker **shouldn't let anyone else know this.** Collect all the pieces of paper.

Players sit in a circle and look around at each other's faces.
The Winker should **wink** at one player at a time without letting anyone else see.

If the Winker winks at **you,** wait five seconds and then **"die" a dramatic death** — this usually requires groaning and falling back out of the circle. **Ham it up!**

If a player thinks he or she has caught the Winker winking at another player, that player should point at the Winker and say **"Winker!"** If the player is right, the game is over. If the player is wrong, he or she is automatically out, and the game continues.

Here's a **joke** from Courtney G. of Ashtabula, Ohio, that we've translated into Ubbi Dubbi:

Whubat hubas fubour
ubeyes bubut cuban't subee?

Answer: Mub issubissubppubi.

42

Back-to-Back Dash

Sent in by Lori R. of Queens, New York.

You will **need** one beach ball or other large ball for each pair.

Ask players to pair up, stand back-to-back, and hook elbows with a partner. Pairs must keep their elbows hooked at all times. One player in each pair holds a ball.

At "Go!" the pairs race toward the finish line as best they can. When they arrive, the player holding the ball must somehow give it to his or her partner to carry on the return trip. The first pair to return to the starting line wins.

P.S. If your group is large, this game works well as a relay.

Toe-to-Toe

Sent in by Gideon and Paul H. of New York City, New York.

Ask players to take off their shoes.

Grab a partner and stand face-to-face.

Hold each other's hands overhead as if you are making a bridge for people to walk under.

Now try to tap the toes of your partner with your toes.

The person who's first to do this three times wins.

P.S.: **No stomping!**

Here's a **joke** from Channell S. of Jamaica Plain, Massachusetts:

If an athlete gets athlete's foot, what does an astronaut get?

Answer: Missile toe.

43

Peanut Push

You will **need** some unshelled peanuts.

Put the peanut on the ground and your hands behind your back.

At "**Go!**" use your **nose** to push or roll the peanut all the way to the finish line.

The first player to push their peanut across wins.

P.S. If your group is large, this game works well as a relay.

Z fact:

Peanuts are one of the world's oldest foods. They originated more than 5,000 years ago in Peru.

Here's a **joke** from Breanne of Schererville, Indiana:

What's the best kind of fish to have with peanut butter?

Answer: Jellyfish.

Mushubeetlayhunnypoo

Mushubeetlayhunnypoo
Is what I always **mutter**,
When my mouth is really full
Of lotsa **peanut butter**.

When I **eat** bananas I yell
Mushallago
And I say
Yommysuga
When I'm **munching** honeydew.

When I **crunch** sugar
cookies,
I say
Icudeeahday.
And when I **chew**
Marshmallows,
It's Loddafloff
I say.

But Mushubeetlayhunnypoo
Is what I always mutter
When my mouth is full
Of lots of **gooey**
Peanut butter!

Hey, Lynese.

Yeah, Zoe?

What's the silliest thing you had to do on ZOOM?

Eat a humongous spoonful of peanut butter. **Mmgfmpf!**

45

Make a Difference

Getting Started

Do you ever watch the news or **read** a story in the newspaper and feel bad about what is happening? You might think that kids can't do anything to make a difference, but they can. *You* can and so can your friends. While it's nice to have *fun* with friends, it can also feel great to accomplish something meaningful together. You and your friends can make a **difference** in your school, your community, and the world.

There are **many ways** you can make a difference:

1. Donate your time and energy. For example, you could tutor a younger student, help clean up a park, or make holiday cards for people in the hospital.

2. Raise money for your cause. For example, you could get pledges for a bike-a-thon or sponsor a car wash.

3. Write a letter or circulate a petition (see samples on pages 49–50).

Here are some **tips** to get you started:

1. Think of things you're **interested in** — like animals, art, the outdoors, sports, cooking, or reading. All of your talents and interests can be put to good use in helping others.

2. Decide how much **time** you realistically have to spend — two hours a week? One Saturday a month?

3. Ask others for **advice** about things you can do to make a difference. Or **read** to find out more about your options. The books on the next page are good places to start.

The Helping Hands Handbook: A Guidebook for Kids Who Want to Help People, Animals, and the World We Live in, by Patricia Adams and Jean Marzollo, illustrated by Jeff Moores; Random House.

It's Our World, Too!: Stories of Young People Who Are Making a Difference, by Phillip Hoose; Little, Brown and Company.

Kids Explore Kids Who Make a Difference, by Westridge Young Writers Workshop; John Muir Publications.

The Kid's Guide to Social Action: How to Solve the Social Problems You Choose — And Turn Creative Thinking into Positive Action, by Barbara A. Lewis; Free Spirit Publishing.

Below are just a few of the many national organizations you might consider contacting about **volunteer opportunities.** There may also be some great local groups you could contact. Who knows — maybe you'll even want to start your own group!

Young America Cares! (YAC!)
United Way of America
701 N. Fairfax Street
Alexandria, VA 22314
(703) 836-7100 (ext. 445)
Helps people in their communities
with various outreach programs.

Habitat for Humanity
121 Habitat Street
Americus, GA 31709-3498
(912) 924-6935
http://www.habitat.org
Organizes volunteers and resources
to build houses for families in need.

March of Dimes
Birth Defects Foundation
1275 Mamaroneck Avenue
White Plains, NY 10605
(914) 428-7100
http://www.modimes.org
Works to prevent birth defects.

Boys & Girls Clubs of America
1230 W. Peachtree Street, NW
Atlanta, GA 30309
(404) 815-5700
http://www.boysandgirlsclubs.org
Works to address a variety of youth
issues.

National Wildlife Federation
8925 Leesburg Pike
Vienna, VA 22184
(703) 790-4000
http://www.nwf.org
Works to protect endangered habitats.

Rainforest Alliance
65 Bleecker Street
New York, NY 10012
(212) 677-1900 or (888) MY EARTH
http://www.rainforest-alliance.org
Works to conserve tropical forests.

Meet Some ZOOMa Cum Laudes

We congratulate and commend these kids for making a real difference — each in his or her own way. Perhaps they will give you and your friends some ideas about things you might like to do.

Lauren L. nominated **Kayla and Kacie D.** of Cayce, South Carolina. Kayla made **candy baskets** for kids who couldn't go trick-or-treating because they were in the hospital on Halloween.

Dot H. of Wabash, Indiana, nominated **Jon and Megan R.** This brother-and-sister team volunteer **four hours a week** at a local children's hospital, going on field trips with kids, taking them for walks, and teaching them crafts.

Malissa B. of Boca Raton, Florida, nominated **Allie, Amy, and David S.** This brother-and-twin-sister team created a campaign called "No Butts About It" to **clean cigarette butts off their beaches.** They hung up 5,000 homemade posters. They want to make Boca Raton the first "butt-free" city in the country.

Cynthia B. of Brookline, Massachusetts, nominated the **Camp Fire Boys and Girls Club** of Brookline. The group raised **more than $3,000** to buy sweatshirts for kids at a homeless shelter.

Dee C. nominated the **Camp Fire Boys and Girls** of Spokane, Washington. As a back-to-school project, these kids collected **1,000 boxes of crayons, 1,000 pencils, 900 notebooks, and 400 erasers** for kids in their town who couldn't afford them.

Write a Letter

You can write a number of different kinds of letters to support an issue you care about. You might write to:

- organizations or individuals who are decision-makers, like your city council members or the owner of a business
- the editor of the school newspaper or local newspaper (Look in the newspaper to see if there are printed guidelines for writing a letter to the editor.)
- a government official (In this case, the best strategy is to ask lots of people to write letters. The more letters received, the more an official will consider your cause a priority.)

Here's an example of how to write a letter. Consider getting an adult to take a look at your letter — he or she might have some valuable suggestions.

Karen Krenitsky [your name]
Any Elementary School [school or group]
Street address
City, State, Zip Code

Date

John Smith [name of person you are writing to]
Commissioner of Parks and Recreation [proper title]
Any Company [company or group]
Street address
City, State + Zip Code

Dear Commissioner Smith:

My name is Karen Krenitsky. I'm in the 4th grade at Any Elementary School. [Identify yourself in your opening.]

I am writing to let you know that the kids on the Southeast side are in real need of a playground and ball field. It's a long trip to the nearest playground on 71st Street, which means we can't stop there on the way home from school. Also, that playground is very crowded. Sometimes you have to wait in a long line to get on the swings or the slide. This year, so many kids signed up for softball and Little League, 100 kids had to be turned away. Shouldn't every kid have a chance to play ball? [State why you are writing.]

There are two large vacant lots on the corner of Main Street and East 34th Street. I think the city should buy this property and build a playground. I'm sure that most of the kids at Any Elementary School and their parents would volunteer to help clean up the lots or even help build the playground. Right now the lots are filled with weeds and trash, and I think a few rats live there. [Suggest a course of action.]

Thanks for your attention to this matter. I look forward to hearing what you think. [You can also say you will call to set up an appointment, if appropriate.]

Sincerely,

Karen Krenitsky [or the names of all the members of your group]

49

Draft a Petition

If you want to bring **attention** to an **issue** and show **decision-makers** that it is important to lots of people, consider passing around a **petition.**

Basically, a petition is a **short letter signed** by lots of people in order to show their **support** for a **cause.** Here's an example of a petition:

Petition for Paper Recycling Program

We, the students of Any Elementary School, think that this school should have a paper recycling program. We are concerned about our environment and think this is one simple thing we can do to protect it.

We recommend that the school put a paper recycling can in every classroom and in the teachers' lounge next to the copy machine. Student volunteers could empty the cans once a week when the paper is taken for recycling.

Name	Address	Phone
1		
2		
3		
4		
5		
6		

Be sure to include your statement at the top of every page, so it is clear that people know what they are signing.

1. Be ready to explain your cause and answer questions when you ask people to sign.

2. Make a copy of your petition before you submit it to the decision-maker, such as the principal or a member of your city council. (You may need the addresses of your supporters later.)

3. If your issue is of community interest, send a copy of your petition to the appropriate local government official.

4. Notify school and/or local reporters when you deliver your petition.

If your petition doesn't force an immediate change, that's okay. Just by writing and circulating the petition you have raised awareness of an issue you feel strongly about.

Top Secret Stuff

Part of being a **friend** is **sharing** secrets. In the pages that follow, you will **learn** some different ways for keeping what's supposed to be **top secret** among friends truly top secret! **Be careful** not to let this book **fall** into **unfriendly hands!**

Invisible Ink

If you want to send **top secret** messages to a friend, consider using invisible ink.

You will need:
• **lemon juice**
• **paper**
• **toothpicks**
• **a toaster**

Ask an adult for help when using the toaster. Lemon juice is your invisible ink. Use a toothpick as you would a pen, dipping it into lemon juice before you **draw** each letter. Let your message dry. The paper will look blank. Send it to a friend. Your friend will be able to **read** your invisible **message** by holding your message very carefully over a warm toaster. (DO NOT LET THE PAPER TOUCH THE TOASTER!!) The heat from the toaster will make the lemon juice turn brown, **revealing** your secret message.

• Meet me at the treehouse at 4:00

Create Your Own Secret Code

A	1
B	2
C	3
D	4
E	5
F	6
G	7
H	8
I	9
J	10
K	11
L	12
M	13
N	14
O	15
P	16
Q	17
R	18
S	19
T	20
U	21
V	22
W	23
X	24
Y	25
Z	26

Have you ever wanted to have your own **secret code?** Just **think** about it: **you** and your **friends** could write each other notes or e-mail using your secret code and **no one else** would be able to read them. Sound like **fun?** Here are **instructions** for developing two secret codes:

Number Code

You can substitute a number for a letter. For example **A = 1, B = 2, C = 3,** and so on. First, make a master code sheet like the one shown here. Write the entire alphabet and each letter's corresponding number. Make sure your friend has a copy, too.

See if you can decipher the following coded messages:

1. 2-5-19-20
   6-18-9-5-14-4-19

2. 23-18-9-20-5 20-15
   26-15-15-13!

Hubey, Jubarubed.

Whubat's thube subillubiubest thubing yubou hubad tubo dubo ubon ZubOOM?

Yubeah, Ubalubisuba?

Ubi hubad tubo drubess ubup lubike Mubiss Ubamuberubicuba. Ubi dubon't knubow ubif ubi'll ubevuber rubecubovuber!

(Answers: 1. Best friends.   2. Write to ZOOM!)

Letter Code

You can also **substitute** one **letter** for another. First, make a **master code** sheet like the one shown here. Write the **entire alphabet,** from A to Z, in one column. Next to A, **start** a column with a **different letter** and **continue** through the alphabet to Z. Start over with A and continue until your **column** is as long as the first one. We started ours with **"H,"** but you could start with any letter.

See if you can decipher these coded messages:

1. AOPZ JVKL PZ JVVS.

2. TLLA TL HMALY ZJVVS.

A	H
B	I
C	J
D	K
E	L
F	M
G	N
H	O
I	P
J	Q
K	R
L	S
M	T
N	U
O	V
P	W
Q	X
R	Y
S	Z
T	A
U	B
V	C
W	D
X	E
Y	F
Z	G

Use the second column as your secret code. Make sure your friend has a copy, too.

Fannee Doolee

likes **zoos** but does not like **animals.** Why do you think that is?

Navajo Code Talkers

In the first years of World War II, the Japanese became very good at deciphering the secret codes of the United States military. Every time the U.S. sent a coded message to its troops, the Japanese were able to break the code and read it almost as quickly as the Americans who received it.

This meant that surprise attacks were not really surprises — the Japanese could read the coded messages that told where and when the Americans would attack. The Americans were in desperate need of a new secret code.

About this time, Philip Johnston, a U.S. civilian and the son of missionaries who had lived among the Navajos, went to the U.S. Marines with an idea. Why not use Navajo as the secret code?

The Navajo language is extremely complex. To speak it, four separate tones of voice must be used: rising, falling, high, and low. The meaning of a word changes depending on the speaker's tone. For instance, the Navajo word for "medicine" and "mouth" look exactly the same — it's just the tone that conveys their different meanings.

Another good reason for using Navajo, thought Johnston, was that very few people (probably about 30) outside of the Navajo tribe could speak the difficult language. He convinced the Marines to recruit the Navajos for this special mission. The Navajos were asked to create a secret code making use of their own language — the U.S. military hoped this would make the code doubly difficult to break.

In order to do this, the Navajos had to invent many new words to describe military terms and inventions. They chose names of things in nature that resembled the military items. For example, the dive bombers looked like sparrow hawks, so they called these "gini," or sparrow hawks; and bombs were sort of like eggs falling from birds, so they called these "a-ye-shi," or eggs.

They also developed an alphabet code so they could spell things if needed, such as place names. To do this, they associated a Navajo word with every letter in the English alphabet. For instance, if they wanted to spell something starting with an "A," they would think of the word "ant" in English and then say its Navajo name, "wol-la-chee."

When the Navajo code talkers were given the chance, they proved the value of their secret code. Several decisive World War II battles, such as those in the Solomon Islands, the Marianas, and at Iwo Jima, utilized the skills of the Navajo code talkers. Military maneuvers succeeded, surprise attacks were carried out, and lives were saved because of the efforts of the Navajo code talkers. The code talkers also enabled the Americans to destroy almost all of the Japanese merchant-marine fleet. This helped to cut off their means for getting wartime supplies.

Over 400 Navajo code talkers served in World War II. Some even served in Korea in the 1950s and Vietnam in the 1960s.

Secret to Ubbi Dubbi Revealed...

At ZOOM we've developed our own secret coded language. We call it Ubbi Dubbi. Here's how it works: Just **add the letters "ub"** before every vowel sound and you, too, can speak Ubbi Dubbi. For instance, if your dog's name is Rover, he becomes Rubovuber. And if your favorite flavor of ice cream is vanilla, it becomes vubanubilluba. Got it? **Grubeat!**

Now go back and see if you can **read** the Ubbi Dubbi in this book — wube wubouldn't wubant yubou tubo mubiss ubout ubon ubanubythubing!

If you have more Ubbi Dubbi questions or want a quick translation, check out the amazing Ubbi Dubbi translator on our Web site at www.pbs.org/zoom. Now you can **ubbify** your e-mail or **dubbify** notes to a friend in mere seconds!

Thubis ubis thube ubend ubof thube bubook. Dubid yubou hubave fubun?

Ubi suebure dubid. Ubin fubact, ubi thubink ubi'll stubart uball ubovuber ubat thube bubegubinnubing!

56

Who Is Fannee Doolee?

boots

shoes

trees

plants

We have another kind of secret code at ZOOM, and we call it Fannee Doolee.

There's a pattern that explains why Fannee Doolee likes and hates the things she does. Fannee Doolee only likes things with **double letters.**

Here's an example: Fannee Doolee loves **sweets but hates candy.** Notice how there are double letters — ee — in *sweets* but none in *candy*? Now that you know why Fannee likes and dislikes what she does, why don't you try to **write your own** Fannee Doolee, and send it to ZOOM!

sweets

candy

Behind the Scenes at  ZOOM™

The **Executive Producer** and **Senior Producer** watch a taped show segment of Alisa to decide if they like the way the segment looks on tape. If they don't like it, they will start over again.

Keiko visits one of the ZOOMers' favorite places in the studio!

The Control Room is where the **Assistant Director** and **Senior Producer** sit and tell the Camerapeople which angles to shoot. The Director picks the camera angle he thinks looks best and then asks the Technical Director, also called the Switcher, to put it on tape.

The **Audio Assistant** puts microphones on the cast members so they can be heard on TV.

The **Makeup Artist** touches up **Pablo's** makeup on the set. The Makeup Artist also does the cast members' hair.

Alisa, David, and the **Executive Producer** do some blocking. Blocking is planning how the segment should go — who should be where and when and doing what.

The Grip, a **Lighting Operator,** and **Pablo** look on as a segment is being prepared for shooting.

Jared hams it up during a rehearsal.

A **Cameraperson** prepares his equipment for taping.

Keiko, Lynese, and **Zoe** goof off between segments.

A segment with **Alisa** is shot.

A computer controls all the lighting on the set. The **Lighting Operator** controls the lights.

The **Props Assistant** gathers material for the next segment. She helps the **Props Coordinator** get together all the stuff that the ZOOMers handle, including materials for ZOOMdos, ZOOMgames, and ZOOMzingers.

Keiko, Alisa, and **Pablo** chill out during a break.

Each cast member's clothes are kept in a pouch labeled with his or her name. This way **Wardrobe** can be sure that each cast member is wearing exactly the same thing every day — from shirts to scrunchies. This is important because one show consists of a number of different segments that are taped on different days. It would look odd if a cast member's shirt changed from one segment to the next on the same show!

The **Audio Director** sits at the mixing board. This is where microphone volumes are adjusted. The Audio Director can listen to everyone's mic at the same time.

The cast together with everyone it takes to create an episode of **ZOOM**.

Here are some other jobs around the set of ZOOM that you might not know about:

The **Grip** sets up lights and makes shadows.

The **Food Stylist** gets the ingredients ready for the CafeZOOM recipes.

The **Jib Cameraperson** operates a camera that's on a long arm.

The **Drama Coach** makes sure the ZOOMers know how to do all the different things they do on the show.

The **Coordinating Producer** selects which ZOOMgames, CafeZOOM recipes, ZOOMzingers, ZOOMdos, and other stuff are done on the show.

The **Research Assistant** tests the ZOOMgames, ZOOMzingers, ZOOMdos, and CafeZOOM recipes. They're tested at the office and with kids at schools and camps to make sure they work, they're fun, and they're not too easy or too hard.

The **Scenics Technician** builds and moves the scenery.

The **Scenics Carpenter** makes sure that the set is in place and looks the very best for the camera.

The **Post Production Assistant** tracks tapes, segments, and other bits and pieces that help the Editors and Post Production Supervisor do what they need to do. He or she also creates the "Znakes" for the shows, the wiggly names you see on-screen.

The **Production Designer** works on the graphic look of the show, coming up with the logo, set design, and ZOOMerangs.

The **Editor** takes the video footage from the studio shoots and pieces them together with music and graphics to create the final ZOOM shows.

Do you know any fun games? Have you written any plays? Do you have any favorite funny jokes? Have you or your friends made a difference in your community or invented your own secret code?

If your answer to any of these questions is yes, please e-mail us at www.pbs.org/zoom or write to us at:

ZOOM
Box 350
Boston, MA 02134

If you send us your ideas, you will receive a free issue of ZOOMerang, and we might put your idea on the show! Don't forget to include your first name, last initial, city, and state.

All submissions become the property of ZOOM and will be eligible for inclusion in all ZOOMmedia. That means that we can share your ideas with other ZOOMers on TV, the Web, in print materials, and in other ZOOM ways.

So, c'mon and send it to ZOOM!